The Life Jesus Chose: Introducing the Spiritual Disciplines

By Dr. Adam W. Christman

Unless otherwise noted, all Scripture quotations are taken from the Christian Standard Bible®, Copyright © 2017 by Holman Bible Publishers. Used by permission. Christian Standard Bible® and CSB® are federally registered trademarks of Holman Bible Publishers.

Copyright © 2025 by Adam W. Christman
All rights reserved.

"The first line in this book says it best – become like Jesus! This kind of life change is a discipleship mandate but seems like an ethereal goal. Fortunately, becoming more like Jesus is the result of implementing simple, yet profoundly transformational spiritual disciplines. As you follow Jesus' example of living these disciplines, you will change at the core of who you are while taking on the character and qualities of Jesus. Read this practical guidebook as a pathway to new dimensions of life in Jesus Christ."

Dr. Jeff Iorg
President, SBC Executive Committee

"Adam Christman has written a timely and significant book. The purpose of the book is outstanding: to encourage readers to live like Jesus did to the best of their ability strengthened by the Holy Spirit. The categories included challenge the readers to think beyond a superficial commitment to God. The easy-to-read style is conversational, born out of years as a pastor. Dr. Christman's passion to be like Jesus is obvious as is his desire to help others as well."

Dr. Rick Melick
Senior Distinguished Professor of New Testament, Gateway Seminary of the Southern Baptist Convention

"Dr. Christman captures joy of serving God and following the example of Christ. He encourages us to embark on this wonderful journey through the same disciplines practiced by Christ when he was on earth. I highly recommend this book for any believer who wants to draw closer to God and follow Christ faithfully."

Peter J. Vik
Pastor, Highpoint Church
Associate Professor of Biblical Studies, San Diego Christian College

Table of Contents

Contents

INTRODUCTION 1

CHAPTER 1: INTENSE STUDY 10

CHAPTER 2: SOLITUDE 22

CHAPTER 3: PRAYER 34

CHAPTER 4: SIMPLE LIVING 46

CHAPTER 5: SERVICE TO OTHERS 62

CHAPTER 6: GATHERING FOR WORSHIP 75

CHAPTER 7: STEWARDSHIP 83

CHAPTER 8: CONFESSION OF SIN 92

CHAPTER 9: CELEBRATION 99

FOR FURTHER READING 107

INTRODUCTION

You can become more like Jesus in your daily living.

I don't mean you can become divine. Rather, I mean you can fulfill God's empowering call from Romans 12:2, "Do not be conformed to this age, but **be transformed** by the renewing of your mind, so that you may discern what is the good, pleasing, and perfect will of God." But we don't seek or need a directionless transformation. We need the best direction to head towards. God also said this in Romans 8:29a, "For those he foreknew he also **predestined to be conformed to the image of his Son**..."

To look like Jesus in our actions, priorities, and choices, and to sound like Jesus in our words and tone of voice, is a tall order. He is perfect and we are not! BUT! Christians do experience change from the old self to the new creation (2 Corinthians 5:17). At the same time, Christians do not make good progress merely by accident or via passive accumulation of godly habits. No, our growth in godliness benefits and abounds as we purposefully and actively seek to become more like our Lord Jesus Christ.

Since our growth to become more Christlike requires our active and purposeful efforts, we utilize the spiritual disciplines.

The spiritual disciplines can be defined as "those behaviors that augment our spiritual growth and enable us to grow to spiritual maturity."[1] I would also phrase them as **following Jesus in the overall style of life He chose for Himself.** In the following pages, I will introduce the spiritual disciplines, arguing for what they are at a broad level and why we need them. The chapters that follow focus in on the spiritual disciplines, one at a time.

Humanity's greatest problem has always been and continues to be a spiritual one. Sin entered the world through the choices of human beings. We perpetuate those choices, ourselves, at an early age. Sin's infection shows itself through things like depression,[2] addiction, anxiety, personal emptiness, consumerism, sex, violence, cultic obsession, and suicide, among other expressions.

---

[1] "What are the spiritual disciplines?" GotQuestions.org, https://www.gotquestions.org/spiritual-disciplines.html, accessed August 19, 2025. That website is a great resource.
[2] Not all depression and anxiety are sin. Work through this with your pastor and a counselor or therapist.

We must take seriously the need for human transformation. We also need to realize and utilize realistic methods of human transformation.

Some think faith *should* make us different all by itself, as long as we don't have to do anything to make it happen. It's called the Fruit of the Spirit, so the Holy Spirit does all the work, right? Well, as with anything having to do with the lives of human beings, God chooses to work *with* you and *through* you. You ever watch Power Rangers? They have this little object called a Morpher. They hold it out after doing a little choreography, say a little something, and poof, they're transformed into their Power Ranger gear and are ready to call down the Zords so they can save the day. God doesn't work like that. Nor does he wave a magic wand over you like Cinderella's fairy godmother. His hand is extended out to you. Take His hand, follow Him, and together you will change your life.

I want to take a brief moment to comment on the Kingdom of God. The Kingdom of God is an ongoing spiritual presence. If your faith is in Christ, you are already in the Kingdom of God. You are already forgiven (Eph. 4:32), redeemed (Eph. 1:7), born again (1 Pet. 1:23), a part of the family of God (Eph. 1:5) and a citizen in the Kingdom of Heaven (Phil. 3:20), among other descriptions. God's presence is with you! Jesus said in the Great Commission, Mt. 28:20, "I am with you always, to the end of the age." Where God is, His Kingdom is. If He is with you, then He stands alongside you, ready to empower you and encourage you as you take at least one step every day in your faith journey.

Now that we know He is with us, we can talk about what His presence and power does for us. We must not take this gracious opportunity lightly or flippantly. Through the spiritual disciplines, you will meet with and dwell with the Triune God! That's an amazing thing! Further, God designed human beings and how we are best to live. Jesus did it perfectly. He mastered it. Just as an apprentice worker benefits from spending time with a master craftsman, we strongly desire to spend time with Jesus to learn from Him. Spending time with Jesus changes things.

G.K. Chesterton was a writer in the 19th and 20th centuries.[2] He famously wrote, "Christianity has not so much been tried and found wanting, as it has been found difficult and left untried." Even as difficult as

Christianity is, we love Jesus. <u>And because we love Jesus, we set our will to resolve to be like Him whom we love.</u>

Jesus said many beautiful things, but I want to highlight one in particular at this point. In Matthew 11:29-30, He said, "Take my yoke upon you and ***learn*** from me, because I am lowly and humble in heart, and you will find rest for your souls. For my yoke is easy and my burden is light" (emphasis added).

Isn't it so interesting that Jesus invites us to *learn* from Him? We all take up a yoke or burden in life. For some of us, the yoke is parental expectations. For others, it is societal expectations. Maybe it is a career goal, or a life goal like living in a certain city, or a certain style of home. Maybe the yoke is to be "free," but eventually we find our so-called "freedom" is a shackle to meaningless or mindless consumption of screens (whether Netflix, gaming, or doomscrolling), sex, or drugs. We all take up a yoke or burden. Why not trade the difficult and heavy yokes of this world for the only one that is easy and light? Joyfully, Christians make that trade. We often mess up and try to pick up the old, heavy burden. But when we repent from sin, we let it drop to the ground again, choosing to continue down the path with our loving Lord.

Not only are you taking up a yoke in your life, one way or another, you will also learn from somebody, somewhere. If we have learned anything from the age of social media, we have learned how powerful and how easy it is for one person to influence another. A meme goes viral and suddenly middle school kids quote it ad infinitum. A young man who is really good at editing silly YouTube videos gets a new haircut and now you can't walk through a store or mall without seeing it dozens of times. Or we see a middle-aged adult share a "life hack" or whatever that is supposed to be some health secret. (Remember the "raw water" trend that popped up from about 2015 to 2019?) More serious examples include isolated individuals who watch and scroll social media for an incredibly unhealthy number of hours, weeks, months, or years, and decide to hurt themselves or others with some action (surgical, sociological, political, or violent) they have convinced themselves to take. My point is, you are going to learn from somebody anyway. And what you put your mind on, you become. Preachers often use the phrase, "You become what you behold," and that is true.

Since you are going to learn from somebody anyway, why not learn from Jesus? Why not learn from the best human being in the history of humanity? The call to learn is right there in Matthew 11:29. He wants to teach you. Will you not learn from Him?

We can learn from Jesus by following Jesus in the overall style of life He chose for Himself. That is, in essence, what the spiritual disciplines are. He told us in John 10:10, "I am come that they might have life, and that they might have it more abundantly." So the way of life He chose for Himself is good. And He knows that His people are called to be like Him. So if we live like He lived (in character, not in technology), we learn from Him as we follow Him.

Let's learn from Jesus. Let's see what HE did so we can see what to emulate.

In the chapters that follow, we will talk about individual spiritual disciplines as practices we can utilize to realistically participate in God's plan for our transformation. The spiritual disciplines include reading the Bible and prayer, as you might expect, but they also include times of (healthy) solitude, living simply, living sacrificially, service to others, confession of sin, celebrating what God has done in your life and the lives of those around you, stewardship, and worship.

Each chapter is organized into a study of how Jesus exemplifies the spiritual discipline of that chapter. We also look to the broader witness of the Bible on that discipline. We also then talk about how you can utilize that discipline in your own life. Scattered at the beginning, end, and in-between the paragraphs of the chapters, are quotes from various Christians who have written about that subject. I hope they are encouraging and enlightening to you, just like they are to me.

Ultimately, I hope this book will be helpful to you as you begin or refine your own practice of the spiritual disciplines so that you might look more like Christ. It is good for you to look like Christ and it is good for the world. We desperately need you to look more like Christ. Everyone benefits as you grow in godliness! I have prepared a list of books for further reading at the end of this book. When you are ready to read something more on this subject, or if you want to see how other thinkers have broken down and discussed the spiritual disciplines, you can turn to those excellent resources.

"Ours is an undisciplined age. The old disciplines are breaking down . . . Above all the discipline of divine grace is derided as legalism or is entirely unknown to a generation that is largely illiterate in the Scriptures. We need the rugged strength of Christian character that can only come from discipline."-V. Raymond Edman

CHAPTER 1: INTENSE STUDY

"Many Christians remain in bondage to fears and anxieties simply because they do not avail themselves of the Discipline of study." -Richard Foster[3]

Do you remember what Jesus said will set us free? Was it good feelings? Maybe, ecstatic experiences? Could it be attending church services? John 8:32 has the answer, "**You will know the truth, and the truth will make you free**" (emphasis added).

Our knowing the truth will set us free. This is one of Jesus' promises to us. The truth will not swoop in like a superhero while we float on the wreckage of life. The truth sits at our elbow, ready and accessible at any moment. We need simply turn and look.

In the introduction of this book, I defined both the spiritual disciplines and, at the same time, any good faith attempt to follow Jesus well, with the statement "**following Jesus in the overall style of life He chose for Himself.**"

---

[3] All Richard Foster quotes come from his book *Celebration of Discipline*. It's a short book and I cannot recommend it enough.

Since we want to follow Jesus in the overall style of life He chose for Himself, we want to look at the behaviors, etc., that we can discover in the eyewitness accounts known as the Gospels of Matthew, Mark, Luke, and John.

Luke 2:52 is a famous passage relevant to this subject. It is simultaneously encouraging, enlightening, and confusing. In it, the Gospel writer reports that Jesus grew "in wisdom and in stature and in favor with God and man." I want you to imagine a baby and how little they know. Imagine a toddler and how little they know. Imagine a grade school kid, a middle school kid, and a high school student, and how little they know. When God the Son put on flesh, he agreed to the whole experience.[2] Jesus was at his conception, is currently, and always will be 100% God and 100% man. He accepted the reality of going through that long growing phase from baby in the womb through all of adolescence to adulthood. Jesus did not come out of the womb preaching the Gospel. He did not teach through parables before he was potty trained. <u>Jesus' need to grow was not a sinful deficiency.</u> <u>It was a matter of biological capacity.</u> He *grew* in wisdom. He really went through the plasticity and growth of the human brain just like the rest of us. And yet, when we get a glimpse of him at age 12, he knows the Scriptures so well he's <u>teaching teachers</u> at the temple. And then when we see him as an adult in the bulk of the Gospel narratives, he knows the Scriptures at a mind-blowing level, both in breadth and in depth. How did he get from here to there? **HE STUDIED.**

One spiritual discipline is the intense study and meditation on God's Word and God's ways.

We study because he studied. We study *hard* because *he studied hard*. And we study because we want to know HIM better. Paul communicated the aim of the Christian life in Philippians 3:10, "**My goal is to know him** and the power of his resurrection and the fellowship of his sufferings, being conformed to his death" (emphasis added). Big brother Paul wanted to know Christ, truly, and increasingly. We want the same. There is no one like Jesus Christ. No one more powerful or peaceful. No one more gracious or gentle. No one so honest or honorable. Nobody has suffered more than Jesus did, nor has anyone been more successful than him (Matt. 16:18). We do not study the Scriptures just to be like him. We study them to know him. Jesus said in John 5:39, "You pore over the Scriptures because you think you have eternal life in them, and yet they testify about me."

Let me quote Richard Foster again. "Study is a specific kind of experience in which through careful attention to reality the mind is enabled to move in a certain direction. Remember, the mind will always take on an order conforming to the order upon which it concentrates." If that is true (and it is), let us concentrate upon the Scriptures to know Jesus better and to become more like him.

Let's also talk about how Jesus treated the Scriptures. We see these actions attested to in the Gospel accounts of his life and actions.

-Jesus treated the Scriptures as historical, not fictional. He refers to the actions that occurred in the Jonah, Moses, and creation (Adam & Eve) stories. He does so in Matthew 12:38-42, Matthew 19:1-12, and Mark 10:6-7 (respectively, though He also refers to the creation/Adam & Eve as history in Matthew 19).

-Jesus treated the Scriptures as authoritative, not suggestive. Another way we could phrase it is that he saw the Scriptures as decisive and binding. In Matthew 5:17-18, he taught, "Don't think that I came to abolish the Law or the

Prophets. I did not come to abolish but to fulfill. For truly I tell you, until heaven and earth pass away, not the smallest letter or one stroke of a letter will pass away from the law until all things are accomplished." Jesus fulfilling the Law is another big subject worthy of its own books. But still we must notice Jesus' respect for the Scriptures as authoritative. In the past, I preached on Matthew 15:1-20, in which Jesus judges the behavior and teachings of the Pharisees as a *breaking* of God's commands (specifically, one of the Ten Commandments). Related to this view of the Scripture is that Christians do not believe anything that is in conflict with the Scriptures. If, for example, every person in the culture around us says, "It is good and right to hate the people that we hate," the Christian stands up and says, "No. Jesus told us to love our neighbors and everyone is my neighbor."

-Jesus treated the Scriptures as rules and support for real world living. Philosophy courses all over the collegiate world read and discuss the Sermon on the Mount (or used to). Though the Sermon on the Mount declares the Kingdom of Heaven, it is largely a lot of ethical teaching, i.e., real world living. And Jesus communicated those teachings as clarifying what God had always meant. After centuries of distortion (intentional and unintentional), Jesus sets the record straight to realign the ethics of God's people with what He had always intended. He continues to do so in other places and times. Matthew 23, for example, shows Jesus addressing the two issues of showing mercy to people and tithes. He says in Mt. 23:23, "Woe to you, scribes and Pharisees, hypocrites! You pay a tenth of mint, dill, and cumin, and yet you have neglected <u>the more important matters of the law</u>--justice, mercy, and faithfulness. <u>These things should have been done without neglecting the others</u>" (emphasis added). Notice, dear reader, that Jesus does not discard the law regarding tithing. Rather, he showed that justice, mercy, and faithfulness are THE MORE IMPORTANT matters. The more important matters of what? They are the more important matters OF THE LAW! There is a rich tapestry to the reality of ethical living in the Scriptures. Jesus points to the law again and again for these practices.

-Jesus treated the coming Scriptures, which you and I call the New Testament, as further revelation on his behalf. More specifically, he believed the Apostles would speak on his behalf. "I still have many things to say to you, but you cannot bear them now. When the Spirit of truth comes, he will guide you into all the truth, for he will not speak on his own authority, but whatever he hears he will speak, and he will declare to you the things that are to come. He will glorify me, for he will take what is mine and declare it to you. All that the Father has is mine; therefore I said that he will take what is mine and declare it to you," John 16:12-15. He knew the Holy Spirit would work in and through certain authors to prepare, compile, write, and edit those books that became the New Testament. And He treated those writings-yet-to-come as glorifying Himself and communicating God's message.

"This is all well and good, Adam, but how do we study?"

Great question! Thank you for asking.

-**Read it**. Regularly, systematically, carefully. Read it regularly by spending at least a few minutes reading it every day. "Intense study" takes more than a few minutes, but you have to start somewhere. When I say "systematically," I mean pick a book of the Bible and start at chapter 1, verse 1. Don't start a new book until you finish that one. If you are new to the Scriptures, I cannot state more strongly that you should start with the Gospel of John. If you need a print Bible and can't afford it, contact your local church. But many free websites exist with translations you can use like the English Standard Version, the Christian Standard Bible, the New American Standard Bible, and more. Finally, when I say read it carefully, I mean we need to read it for what it is. Every book has one or more genre, cultural contexts, and other factors to ultimately account for. This part of reading the Bible is the hardest and will require that we help one another do it well. And let me encourage you with another piece of advice. If you're just starting out, simply read it and trust it by faith. You will learn more in time. Don't worry about becoming an "expert" first.

Let me add, <u>you must truly read it for yourself</u>. I am aware of AI apps that will summarize any book you want. Not only are these apps untrustworthy from the start, it robs you of the point of reading. The point of reading the book is to best grapple with an argument, if nonfiction, or to best grapple with the themes and questions raised by the narrative, if fiction. With the Bible, reading it for yourself becomes even more important! You are reading this unique book written by God Himself in order to know the truth so that you might be set free! How will you know the truth if you use AI summaries that are completely unreliable? You won't. And the more atheistic or other unbelieving programmers and tech companies run things, the less reliable the summaries of the Bible will be. The same thing will also be true of helpful Christian books like Mere Christianity. Would you have AI summarize a love note from your spouse? Would you have AI summarize what it is like to witness the birth of a child? Would you have AI summarize the weight and meaning of your presence as you sit or stand in honor of a loved one in their final moments? As Augustine heard in the garden that day, "Take up, and read."

-**Learn about genre**. Gospel, history (e.g., Acts), epistles, apocalyptic, prophetic, Law, poetry. Each one has features and flavor that are unique and will impact The Author's meaning.

-**Learn some cultural context stuff**. Sounds technical, huh? Some of these things may not seem important, but they will add flavor. Let me give you an example from the Gospel of John. In John 8:12, Jesus identifies Himself as "the light of the world." You can read that passage and that whole Gospel and understand that statement perfectly well. No problem. And yet! If you knew about the Feast of Tabernacles they were observing at that time, and if you knew about the lamps they would light in the temple as a part of that festival, and if you knew that they celebrate that feast and they light those lamps as a celebration and reminder of God's great gracious act of leading them in the exodus from Egypt as a pillar of fire (which is, of course, a light source...), there is a richness and depth you would miss without that knowledge. Let me put it this way. You don't want to eat boiled chicken and steamed broccoli for every meal, do you? Don't you want more flavor, more zest? Don't you want to experience the full richness of what you can experience, like a well-seasoned BBQ chicken thigh, or a steak cooked with butter and seasonings in a cast iron skillet? Graduate from only "the milk" to also "the meat" over time.

-**Look for and see how the Scripture connects to itself**. In other words, *let the Bible tell you about itself!* When you are confused, be kind to yourself because you won't understand everything on the first read. Also keep in mind that Scripture interprets Scripture. Look for prophecies pronounced, then fulfilled.

Look for promises made and promises kept. Learn about and look for foreshadowing, aka typology. Some pieces you will have to work harder for, but others are made very plain by the revelation of Jesus' own words, or the words of the Apostles, like in the book of Hebrews when it tells us about Jesus being in the priesthood according to Melchizedek. That is a confusing passage at first, second, maybe even at the twentieth read. But keep looking. Don't give up!

-**Keep navigating by the north star of Scripture that all the Scriptures speak of Jesus**. You will get confused and you will have questions. Both of those things are perfectly fine. God is big enough to handle that and He has more than enough love for you to be patient with you through those times. At the same time, look for Jesus in every book of the Bible. As a long, long-time reader of the Bible, I can tell you: He's there.

For Further Reading:

- *The Story Retold: A Biblical-Theological Introduction to the New Testament*, by G.K. Beale and Benjamin L. Gladd.

- *Grasping God's Word*, by J. Scott Duvall and J. Daniel Hays. Available in hardcover and digital.

- *How to Read a Book: The Classic Guide to Intelligent Reading*, by Morimer J. Adler and Charles Van Doren.

- *Exegetical Fallacies*, by D.A. Carson.

- *Holman Bible Atlas: A Complete Guide to the Expansive Geography of Biblical History*, edited by Thomas V. Brisco.

- *Dictionary of New Testament Background*, edited by Craig A. Evans and Stanley E. Porter Jr., The IVP Bible Dictionary Series. (There are others in this series relating to the Old Testament, or specifically the Gospels, for example.)

CHAPTER 2: SOLITUDE

"All of humanity's problems stem from man's inability to sit quietly in a room alone." -Blaise Pascal (1623–1662)

The introverts reading this book may already be cheering. I'll pretend I can faintly hear you from this distance! Solitude? Spending time by myself? "Sign me up," you quietly say as you turn the pages of this book. In a busy world, we are all pulled away from this healthy practice by the demands of work, family, friends, and more. But solitude is much more than simply alone time and it is certainly different from doomscrolling alone in your bed at night.

I want to remind you that we have defined the spiritual disciplines and, at the same time, any good faith attempt to follow Jesus well, with the statement "**following Jesus in the overall style of life He chose for Himself**."

There is much that can and should be said about all the spiritual disciplines, but the chapters of this book are focused introductions that spotlight our Lord Jesus and how we can learn these disciplines from Him. He is the only perfect person in all of human history, so those of us who know how very, very good He is desire to become like Him in our character.

Also, human transformation (changed lives) really can happen. I've seen it happen and I've experienced it.

Solitude is a purposeful time spent with God.

Solitude (and, with it, times of silence) is an old spiritual discipline that does connect back to Jesus' own practices that we can see in the Gospels. Again, solitude, *as a spiritual discipline*, is more than being alone. Rather, **solitude is a purposeful time spent with God**. In many instances, you may spend that time with Christian music playing where you can hear it, even if only faintly. You may spend that time praying aloud to him. But in other instances, you might pray silently and hold back from talking out loud to yourself. (I do encourage you to consider engaging in a time of *silent* solitude from time to time.)

Let's briefly look at five instances where Jesus spent a period of time in solitude and, potentially, silence. Though each instance is a period of *purposeful* solitude, each instance will be for a *different* purpose.

Jesus spent time in solitude in order to prepare for a major task.

Luke 4:1-15. This passage is Luke's account of Jesus' famous temptation by Satan himself. It comes right after Jesus' baptism by his cousin John the Baptist in the Jordan river. Luke 4:1-2 say, "Then Jesus left the Jordan, full of the Holy Spirit, and was led by the Spirit in the wilderness for forty days to be tempted by the devil. He ate nothing during those days, and when they were over, he was hungry."

Between the account in Luke's Gospel and the one in Matthew's Gospel, we can see that Jesus does not have his disciples because he has not called them yet. He is completely, one-hundred percent on his own in the wilderness. He participates in this to test himself against the temptations of the Tempter-in-Chief, the Original Tempter, Satan. How well would you and I do against the temptations of Satan if he, personally, were the demon testing us? And what if you and I were each on our own for 40 entire days, no cell phone, and worst of all no food? I don't know about you, but I might fold pretty quickly. Jesus, though, proves His character not simply to Himself, but to the world by resisting every temptation!

In Luke 4, Jesus spent time in solitude in order to prepare for a major task. Specifically, the beginning of his public ministry. As you read, you will see that his return to society leads directly into ministry (Luke 4:14-15) and, soon after (Luke 5), the calling of His first disciples.

You and I have major tasks in our lives. We begin a new job. Or we begin a new project at work. Maybe you are about to begin the active stewardship of an aging or ailing loved one who needs regular or constant care. That's a major task! If Jesus spent some time in solitude, it would be wise for you and I to do the same.

Jesus spent time in solitude to rest and, after the death of his cousin, to grieve.

In the Gospel of Mark, we see another instance of Jesus seeking a time of solitude. Chapter 6 reports the tragic death of His cousin, John the Baptist. When that happens, Jesus hears about it through John's disciples (Matt. 14:12). In this period where He would obviously grieve John's death, as well as the manner of his death, Jesus seeks time alone (Mark 6:32), but the crowds find Him. In His great compassion, Jesus puts off rest and serves the crowds by teaching them and ultimately feeding the five thousand.

After the feeding of the five thousand, Jesus sends the crowds home and He also sends the disciples on to Bethsaida by a boat. Mark 6:45-47 shows us, "Immediately he made his disciples get into the boat and go ahead of him to the other side, to Bethsaida, while he dismissed the crowd. After he said good-bye to them, he went away to the mountain to pray. Well into the night, the boat was in the middle of the sea, and he was alone on the land." In other words, when the work was done, Jesus spent time alone to rest or recharge, as well as to grieve. Please do not mistake my point: not all grieving can or even should be done in solitude. Let the church help you carry your burden (Gal. 6:2)! The point I hope you are seeing is that even Jesus, the only perfect person, chose to prioritize having times of solitude to rest after hard work and in order to grieve.

Notice also that "he went away to the mountain **_to pray_**" (emphasis added). His solitude for rest and grief was not "alone time." In fact, he was spending time with someone: Jesus spent time in prayer with God the Father. When was the last time you spent alone time with God instead of with your phone? I don't mean 5 or 15 minutes in the morning before you go to work. When was the last time you took real time out of your schedule to devote it to one-on-one time with the Lord? Jesus did it. Let's learn from Him (Matt. 11:29).

Jesus spent time in solitude before making an important decision.

Turning back to Luke, we find Jesus spending time in solitude before making an important decision. Luke 6:12-13 tells us about that moment. "During those days he went out to the mountain to pray and spent all night in prayer to God. When daylight came, he summoned his disciples, and he chose twelve of them, whom he also named apostles."

We know from Luke's Gospel that Jesus has already engaged in truth-telling and preaching. So this time of solitude is distinct from the kind where He prepared for a major task, as discussed above regarding Luke chapter 4. Rather than a major task, this solitude precedes an important decision or question: who will be the twelves disciples raised to a special level of Jesus' investment in terms of time and mentoring (discipleship)? Time alone with God allowed Jesus the space of prayer and "unhurriedness" to come to peaceful clarity.

Who amongst us could not use peaceful clarity when making an important decision? Do you remember the last time you were rushed into a truly important decision? It was pretty awful, right? And you might have made the wrong decision in the moment, where you selected an option that seemed good at that time, but when you had more time to consider you realize it was not the wisest or best option. Consider this. Even Jesus needed time alone with God before making an important decision. We are not better or wiser than Jesus. Surely, we need time alone with God before making important decisions, too.

Jesus spent time in solitude during a time of stress (or, distress).

Luke 22 is a powerful and important chapter. Amongst other important parts of the life of Jesus, Luke records another time of solitude, spent for a different purpose than the others we have examined so far.

Luke 22:39-44 reports on Jesus' time in solitary prayer on the Mount of Olives just prior to Judas' betrayal and the arrest of Jesus. (The entire moment covers verses 39-46 before rolling into Judas' betrayal in verse 47.) Here are the verses: "He went out and made his way as usual to the Mount of Olives, and the disciples followed him. When he reached the place, he told them, 'Pray that you may not fall into temptation.' Then he withdrew from them about a stone's throw, knelt down, and began to pray, 'Father, if you are willing, take this cup away from me — nevertheless, not my will, but yours, be done.' Then an angel from heaven appeared to him, strengthening him. Being in anguish, he prayed more fervently, and his sweat became like drops of blood falling to the ground."

You may already know that by this time in Jesus' life, He is abundantly aware of what He is about to experience at the hands of the religious leaders and the Romans. He knows the Messiah is to also be the Suffering Servant, who would bear the earthly weight of physical beatings and literal bodily death. He knows that He is the Lamb of God who takes away the sin of the world. He knows that this Lamb is a sacrificial lamb, who will come to be known as the Lamb Who Was Slain. Jesus had to die because the wages of sin is death, which is to say Jesus would bear the heavenly weight of the wrath of God. He would receive in His person the righteous penalty for all the sins of every man, woman, boy, and girl who would put their faith in Him. He knew the burden to come. Further, Jesus is both God and man. As a human being, He felt what any other human being would feel in that context. He felt stressed. He felt so stressed that the Gospel reports Him sweating blood (Luke 22:44).

So, stop and look at what Luke is reporting to us. Jesus felt stress, incredibly high levels of stress considering His near future. What is He to do? Blow off steam with a game? Numb the stress with alcohol or mind-altering substances? No. This person is Jesus. He took that opportunity to spend time in solitude during a time of stress.

Jesus' solitude during this time of stress served the purpose of remembering both God's will and God's mission. God's will was that He Himself would bear the sins of His people. The judge would get off the judgment seat and put himself in the execution chamber to take the death penalty for the convicted criminal. God's mission is to seek and to save the lost (Luke 19:10). But He can't do much seeking or saving if He doesn't die for the sins of His people. So Jesus' time of solitude is clearly a time of prayer (Lk. 22:41-42) and it is a time where He can clarify those two issues. There is no doubt in my mind that Jesus sought this time in order to walk with peace, strength, and dignity through His betrayal, trials, sufferings, and death.

Maybe this example is the easiest pill to swallow. It is common practice even for people who don't consider themselves Christians to pray to God for help during times of trouble. There is a popular song on the radio nowadays where the American theologian singer and guest wrestler on WWE Jelly Roll says, "I only talk to God when I need a favor, and I only pray when I ain't got a prayer." My point here is not to speak against this practice, but rather to encourage it. Pray at all times (1 Thess. 5:17). But when the times are tough, you have to turn to your Heavenly Father. If anyone has help for you and a way out, it is Him.

Jesus *often* spent time in solitude in order to pray.

We have come to our last passage. I know we have spent a lot of time in the Gospel of Luke, but go into it with me one more time. In Luke 5:15-16, we read about Jesus' practice after ministry efforts. Those verses tell us, "But the news about him spread even more, and large crowds would come together to hear him and to be healed of their sicknesses. Yet he often withdrew to deserted places and prayed."

I certainly hope you will notice that Jesus uses times of solitude and prayer to rest. Notice, it shows him having times of true solitude, not simply time apart from the crowds with His disciples. But I hope you will especially notice in this passage the powerful little adverb "often." Jesus "often" withdrew to deserted places to pray, it says. How incredible is that? I know it can be hard to imagine or wrap your brain around it, but Jesus really did spend relatively frequent times of solitude for the purpose of prayer. We can barely squeeze in 5 minutes of Bible reading a day, while also spending countless hours listening to podcasts, debating the finer points of our favorite baseball team, or catching up on two to five hours of whatever show has our attention lately. Jesus's frequent habit of solitude for the purpose of prayer may be a wake-up call kind of challenge, but I think it is the one we need.

"But this is Jesus we're talking about," you object. You would be right in that objection if you mean we cannot achieve perfection through our efforts. Jesus, however, calls us to "learn" from him (Matt. 11:29). And we can become like him if we will continue to "**follow Jesus in the overall style of life He chose for Himself**." He did it. We can do it. Let's do it!

Allow me to close with one more question and response. Are any of the situations I described in this chapter unique to Jesus? Of course not. We all prepare for major tasks, return from hard work, grieve losses, prepare to make important decisions, experience stress, and need to pray. None of us are immune from these challenges of life. If we will spend time alone with God, He will guide, encourage, and provide for us like He has done before.

Sometime soon (maybe today) turn off your phone. Put away the work project. Ask someone to watch the kids for a little bit. And find time to be genuinely alone with the Lord God. He wants you to spend time with Him. He wants you to know Him better. He wants you to take up His yoke and burden. He wants you to learn from Him! He wants to bless you. So take some time very soon and spend it alone. Spend it alone with God and spend it purposefully, for the sake of the richness of your life in Christ.

CHAPTER 3: PRAYER

"It is not enough for the believer to begin to pray, nor to pray correctly; nor is it enough to continue for a time to pray. We must patiently, believingly continue in prayer until we obtain an answer. Further, we have not only to continue in prayer until the end, but we have also to believe that God does hear us and will answer our prayers. Most frequently we fail in not continuing in prayer until the blessing is obtained, and in not expecting the blessing. Those who are disciples of the Lord Jesus should labor with all their might in the work of God as if everything depended upon their own endeavors. Yet, having done so, they should not in the least trust in their labor and efforts, nor in the means that they use for the spread of the truth, but in God alone; and they should with all earnestness seek the blessing of God in persevering, patient, and believing prayer. Here is the great secret of success, my Christian reader. Work with all your might, but never trust in your work. Pray with all your might for the blessing in God, but work at the same time with all diligence, with all patience, with all perseverance. Pray, then, and work. Work and pray. And still again pray, and then work. And so on, all the days of your life. The result will surely be abundant blessing.

Whether you see much fruit or little fruit, such kind of service will be blessed." -George Muller, 1805-1898

Now that you are a Christian, what is the most important thing you can do? If you took a survey with that question, you might hear responses like "evangelism" or "worship." I wonder how often you would hear "pray."

Prayer can feel very passive. Isolated. When you are new to the practice of prayer, or perhaps during some of the harder times of life, you can feel like you're sending out signals into an unanswering universe. Jesus wants you to know that this perspective on prayer is not accurate and it is not what He intends for your life.

Earlier in this book, I defined the disciplines as "those behaviors that augment our spiritual growth and enable us to grow to spiritual maturity." I also offered that these disciplines are **"following Jesus in the overall style of life He chose for Himself."** Engaging in the spiritual disciplines is for the human soul what watering, pruning, and fertilizing is to a plant. It is the way Jesus modeled how to engage the process of human growth and, for us, transformation. Author Richard J. Foster said,

"To pray is to change. Prayer is the central avenue God uses to transform us. If we are unwilling to change, we will abandon prayer as a noticeable characteristic of our lives."

Jesus chose a lifestyle of prayer. More specifically, he chose to pray in the morning, during the day, and at night. He chose to pray alone and in groups. He prayed while fasting and He assumed His followers would fast. He commanded His followers to pray. He modeled prayer and explicitly taught us how to pray. So we see He took a variety of approaches to prayer, rather than one, lone model of prayer. We also see that He both modeled and commanded prayer for us to engage.

Richard Foster wrote, "Of all the Spiritual Disciplines prayer is the most central because it ushers us into perpetual communion with the Father." Based on what I've read in the Bible and my own experiences, I find that quote to be accurate. Pastor and author H.B. Charles Jr. defines prayer this way, "Prayer reflects our confidence in the heavenly Father to care for our needs."[4] Prayer is a method of spending time with God, of us communicating to Him and

---

[4] H.B. Charles, Jr., *It Happens After Prayer: Biblical Motivation for Believing Prayer*, Chicago: Moody Publishers, 2013.

Him communicating to us. While it is a rare experience to hear an audible voice, God's communication to us is real and discernible.

In the rest of this chapter, I will examine multiple passages from the eyewitness accounts of Jesus' life to see the elements of Jesus' various styles of prayer. Rather than list them all out as I did in the previous paragraph, they will occur together. I'm sure you will see the same thing I see in them.

The Gospel of Mark, chapter 1, shows us several elements to Jesus' prayer on a certain day. Jesus had just spent all day healing people and exorcising demons for "the whole town" (Mark 1:33), possibly into the night. Mark 1:35 then says, "Very early in the morning, while it was still dark, he got up, went out, and made his way to a deserted place; and there he was praying." I have noticed five elements in this verse. Do you see them, too?

One element of Jesus' prayer on this day is that it was <u>early in the morning</u>. The text makes this very plain. I am reminded of a famous quote from the Protestant Reformer Martin Luther, who said, "If I fail to spend two hours in prayer each morning, the devil gets the victory through the day. I have so much business I cannot get on without spending three hours daily in prayer." Luther's habit was to start his day with two hours of prayer, but if he was especially busy, he devoted THREE hours to prayer instead. This choice seems backward to me as a busy, 21st century American. But the more I know the Lord and the more I know the use of prayer, the more I see the wisdom in it. Jesus likely spent significant time in prayer (more on that in a moment). He knew He needed it. If GOD THE SON needed to pray before He started his day, how much more do you and I need to do the same?

A second element of Jesus' prayer on this day in Mark 1:35 is that <u>He prayed by Himself</u>. Notice, it said "he" got up and went out. Not "they." He was unaccompanied by His disciples or family members. Praying in groups is good and right and commanded in the New Testament. But you will benefit greatly from consistent, regular prayer where you are alone with God. He wants you, individually, to know Him. He wants your heart (yours, specifically) aligned with His. And He wants to guide your steps as you go on your own life's journey. It is difficult in our busy schedules to find time to pray alone. It is tempting to get on our phones or do something else for dopamine. But consistent, regular prayer will result in rich times spent with God. I have experienced this truth in my life. I know you can experience it, too. Luke 5:16 also reports that this style of prayer was a regular occurrence for Jesus, "Yet he *often* withdrew to deserted places and prayed" (emphasis added).

A third element of Jesus' prayer on this day is <u>He prayed for a lengthy period of time</u>. He was apparently gone so long, the disciples had to go look for Him. We find this in Mark 1:36-37, the following verses. "Simon and his companions searched for him, and when they found him they said, 'Everyone is looking for you.'" If everyone was looking for Jesus, then enough of the morning had passed that people were up, dressed, had eaten their breakfast, and possibly had done their morning chores in order to be freed up to go find this miracle worker who might do something amazing right before their eyes. As they were looking for Jesus, they probably came to the house that hosted Jesus and the disciples the night before. And so the disciples were motivated to get outside and find Jesus! They found Him having spent a significant amount of time in prayer. That kind of behavior may not seem possible for you right now. But what if you chose the true rest of prayer over the leisure of Netflix? Are there blocks of time you spend on things that either can wait or that you do not actually need? Could you not re-allocate some of that to a regular prayer time? Time spent in prayer is never time wasted.

A fourth element of Jesus' prayer on this day is that <u>He chose prayer over ministry</u>. That might sound crazy, but look at the biblical text. We get this observation from the fuller passage, Mark 1:35-38. Here is verse 38: "And [Jesus] said to them, 'Let's go on to the neighboring villages *so that I may preach there too*. This is why I have come'" (emphasis added). Jesus COULD have been performing acts of ministry already on this day. He knew that Capernaum had plenty of people in and around it. He knew there would be more people who were ill. The people of Capernaum were the reason the disciples went and found Jesus praying alone! We know from verse 37 that the disciples had just told Jesus that everyone was looking for Him. So Jesus did not leave Capernaum due to an assumption that there was no longer any need in that town. We know, instead, that His primary mission was to preach the Gospel. Rather than spend every possible minute in acts of ministry, He chose to connect with God in prayer in order to best fulfill His ministry. You might even say He left ministry opportunities in order to go pray.

The fifth element of Jesus' prayer on this day is that He prayed before the difficult work of ministry. The following passage, in fact the next verse, Mark 1:39, says, "He went into all of Galilee, preaching in their synagogues and driving out demons." He transitions from a lengthy time of solitary prayer into a period of ministry service that cost Him time and energy. Mark 1:39 probably refers to a period of multiple days, if not weeks. Do you jump into acts of ministry without praying beforehand? My friend, don't do this to yourself. You could be so much more encouraged, invigorated, strengthened, and ready for the task at hand if you would pray first.

"Prayer—secret, fervent, believing prayer—lies at the root of all personal godliness." -William Carey, 1761-1834

Let us turn to a few more passages from the life of Jesus to see how He handled prayer.

While Jesus did pray alone many times, He also prayed with others. We see this in a variety of passages, including the Sermon on the Mount (Matthew 6) and the Last Supper (e.g., Luke 22:17, 19).

Jesus modeled prayer. He showed how to pray at His baptism in Luke 3:21. He laid His hands on children and prayed for them in front of the disciples in Matthew 19:13. He prayed privately, but His disciples were with Him during His individual prayer time in Luke 9:18. He told the disciples of His prayers for them. The Lord tells Peter, for example, of His prayers for Him in Luke 22:32. John 17 is a prayer for His disciples and is prayed in their hearing.

He modeled prayer, but He also gave explicit instructions on how to pray. He taught us how to pray in terms of *content* in Matthew 6:9-13. That prayer is popularly known as "the Lord's Prayer," but some (myself included) have taken to calling it "the Model Prayer." It is a prayer that WE, the disciples of Jesus, are to pray. Jesus has no debts or need for forgiveness. Those elements in the Model Prayer show that it is really a prayer for us to pray, not His prayer to pray. Directly before the Model Prayer, however, Jesus also taught us the *posture* of prayer we are to have in Matthew 6:5-8. As you read that passage, you will notice that the posture is not so much whether our bodies are lying down, sitting down, standing up, etc. The posture of prayer is one of sincerity, if I can use a simple term to sum up His teaching in those verses.

Jesus modeled and assumed His disciples would fast. Matthew 4 famously reports the temptations of Christ by the devil at the end of a forty-day period where Jesus modeled fasting and solitude. The Sermon on the Mount shows us that Jesus assumes we will fast when He says, "Whenever you fast..." He does not say "if." He assumes that we will take up the practice of occasional denial for the purpose of dwelling on the truth that God is always and only our source of provision.[5]

<u>Jesus commanded us to pray</u>. This fact makes prayer nonnegotiable for Christians. The joy of it is, though, that prayer is no begrudging duty.

---

[5] You may have dietary or other health complications that may change, limit, or prohibit your ability to engage in traditional fasting from food. If you think this may describe you, ask your physician if there is a form of fasting from food or drink that you CAN engage. If you cannot engage in fasting from food or drink in any way due to your dietary or health needs, feel free to contact me at my website and I'll be happy to make some suggestions that do not impact your diet or health in a negative way. You can, for example, change a habit. Instead of watching TV for the last hour of your day, you can give that time to God by spending it reading or more intensely studying the Bible.

It is a powerful privilege to enter the presence of God, knowingly. God told Moses, "No one may see me and live" (Exodus 33:20). But now we have Jesus, Immanuel, God With Us. At the end of prayer we walk away unscathed, but not unchanged.

He commanded us to pray in such strong terms that He even told us to love and pray for our enemies in Matthew 5:43-44.

Prayer changes us. It aligns our hearts with God's heart as we spend time with Him. Prayer is our walkie talkie as soldiers in the field reaching out to our commanding officer for orders. And prayer changes things (James 1:5). I hope you see the need for daily—or more accurately, constant (1 Thess. 5:17)—prayer.

I want to close with a story I read in H.B. Charles Jr.'s book.

A father and his son were riding their bikes together one day. As they rode down the trail, the father eyed a large branch that had fallen in the path ahead. Instead of riding around it, the father decided to use this as an opportunity to teach his son an important lesson. They pulled over, and the father instructed his son to move the branch out of the way.

The boy pushed and pulled, but was unable to move the branch. "I can't do it," he said, exhausted. "Sure you can, Son," replied the father. "Be sure to use all your strength." The boy tried harder. But he could not move the branch.

Near tears, he said again, "I can't do it."

"Did you use all of your strength?" The father asked.

"Yes," the boy answered.

"No you didn't," the father replied. "You didn't ask me to help you."

For Further Reading:

- H.B. Charles, Jr. *It Happens After Prayer: Biblical Motivation for Believing Prayer.*
- Dallas Willard, *The Divine Conspiracy.*

CHAPTER 4: SIMPLE LIVING

"Simplicity is freedom. Duplicity is bondage. Simplicity brings joy and balance. Duplicity brings anxiety and fear." -Richard J. Foster

The Bible has much to say about the spiritual disciplines across the breadth of its books, but these chapters have zeroed in on the life and teachings of Jesus. I do not elevate the words of Jesus over and against the rest of Scripture. ALL of Scripture is God-breathed, after all. Instead, we are focusing on a more narrow target for the sake of brevity. It may be of more help to Christians who are new to the disciplines to begin with a narrow focus before moving to a broader study of what the rest of the Bible says about these practices.

Simple living is a spiritual discipline. Though it looks a little different than the intense study of God's Word, or the frequent prayers of a Christian, it is still commanded by Christ. He designed and intends it for our flourishing! Simple living in the biblical sense is not a plaid-wearing, John Denver-listening country farm house away from the bustle of an urban center as packaged and sold to us by so many people on TV and the internet.[6] Nor is simple living just some form of minimalism. Marie Kondo is not the mouthpiece of Jesus on this issue. (Is a meme from 2019 too old a reference?) Simple living is also not a form of transcendentalism or trying to elevate the spiritual over the physical. Jesus has too much interest in the physical to be a true transcendentalist. The early church knew transcendentalists as Gnostics and rightly rejected the philosophical divisions they attempted to put between the spiritual and the physical.

Some of Christian ethics is commanded by Jesus and some is modeled by Him. The subject of simple living follows that pattern. Some simple living is commanded, but some is modeled and NOT commanded. Since the list of that which is modeled but not commanded is shorter, I will begin there before turning to the list of Jesus' commands with regards to simple living. I will conclude with a definition of simple living based on the life and teachings of Jesus.

The biggest example of an element of simple living in the life of Jesus that is NOT commanded is that Jesus had no home.

---

[6] It is no sin to thank God that you're a country boy, but Jesus has something richer and more meaningful in mind for us than John Denver.

Matthew 8:20 reports the words of Jesus. It is not a command, but a description, "Jesus told him, 'Foxes have dens, and birds of the sky have nests, but the Son of Man has no place to lay his head.'" The context of these words is a brief passage where two men claim to want to follow Jesus but would like to delay following Him. In another passage, Jesus responds to one described as a scribe (Mt. 10:19) where He declares He has no place to lay His head. Again, this statement is descriptive, not an imperative. He does not command His disciples to become or remain homeless. However! It has been true that some Christians will lose their homes as a result of following Jesus. I've known people who have been rejected from their families and their literal homes for choosing to follow Jesus as a Christian. Such experiences will continue and may only increase between now and the return of Jesus. But Jesus does not *command* our homelessness. He has come that we might have life, and life abundantly (John 10:10). He would know the negative impacts of such an experience on most people.[7] Other

---

[7] Many studies, for decades, have shown the negative effects of homelessness on mental health. Deborah K. Padgett, "Homelessness, housing instability and mental health: making the connections," *BJPsych Bulletin* 44(5),

suggestions may be made, but this example of simple living that Jesus modeled and yet did not command will suffice for now.

The next, and the largest, section of this week's post looks at elements or ways of simple living that incorporate both Jesus' modeling and His commands.

Jesus took very little with Him on His journeys and encouraged His disciples to do the same. We see His words on this element in Matthew 10:10 and Luke 10:4. Look in the Gospels for how Jesus traveled. Did He do so with an elaborate train of support staff, creature comforts, and riches? Certainly not. In Matthew 10:10, He told His disciples, "Don't take a traveling bag for the road, or an extra shirt, sandals, or a staff, for the worker is worthy of his food." Oh no! I can hear you saying. "I can only travel with the clothes on my back??" Looking at the context of Matthew 10 helps us see that this sending is a special sending for the 12 disciples/soon-to-be-apostles. But there is wisdom here that is applicable to all Christians. Let me give you an example. All the

---

2020 Oct. See also PT Fischer and WR Breakey, "Homelessness and mental health: an overview," *International Journal of Mental Health* 14, 1985: 6–41.

missionaries I have known do not pack up some ten-room house and move hundreds of pounds of belongings overseas or across the nation to share the Gospel. Often, they have a few bags of clothes and cherished possessions, then buy what they need once they arrive. This practice is right in line with the Sermon on the Mount in Mt. 6:19-24. In those verses, Jesus urges us not to treasure the things of this world, but to store up treasures in heaven. He warns us not to try to serve both God and mammon (aka, money). We can easily and quickly find so-called pastors on YouTube and social media who do not embody simple living with their expensive watches, clothes, cars, and private jets. But remember, pastors are not held to a higher standard! We hold pastors to the Christian standard; we just hold them to it more rigorously.

Jesus taught against greed in the Sermon on the Mount, but also in Matthew 19:16-30. The Rich Young Ruler approached Jesus, asking after eternal life. He even claims to Jesus that he has kept "all" the commandments (Mt. 19:20; check for yourself if you don't belive me; its a bold claim!). Jesus tells the young man to sell his belongings and the young man walked away grieving! The Rich Young Ruler does not embody simple living. We should take his example as a warning. How much stuff do we really need? How much do we really need in our bank account? If our family is cared for by having all our needs and some of our wants, is that not enough? Can it be true that simply having all our family's needs covered is enough?[8]

"Simplicity sets possessions in proper perspective." -Richard Foster

Jesus taught against greed, but we also see in His example that He sacrificed earthly gain. In John 7, Jesus' brothers come to Him with a proposal. They believed that He could heal after seeing Him do it again and again. But they did not believe in Him. And there is a big difference! His brothers urge Jesus to go to the Feast of Booths in Jerusalem and show off! If He did so, He would perform in front of huge crowds and could maybe get a lot of money, power, and earthly influence. Instead, Jesus delays (Jn. 7:9-10). When He does go, Jesus

---

[8] Dallas Willard has much to say about this in his book *The Spirit of the Disciplines*. For example, "The idealization of poverty is *one of the most dangerous illusions of Christians in the contemporary world*. Stewardship—which requires possessions and includes giving—is the true spiritual discipline in relation to wealth" (emphasis in original; page 194).

does no miracles. Instead, He teaches the crowds and debates the Pharisees. He continues to live simply, seeking no earthly riches, power, or influence. His Kingdom is different.

"But those who want to be rich fall into temptation, a trap, and many foolish and harmful desires, which plunge people into ruin and destruction," 1 Timothy 6:9.

Jesus' ethics are simple, but far-reaching: Love God, Love Others. Simple! But they touch on everything and everyone in life.

Simple living impacts our speech. In the Sermon on the Mount, Jesus says, "But let your 'yes' mean 'yes,' and your 'no' mean 'no.' Anything more than this is from the evil one" (Matthew 5:37). If anyone on the face of the planet in 2025 speaks honestly with the most frequency, it better be Christians. Aren't you tired of Christians lying? Or "twisting the truth"? Why must we act that way? Can we not live a better way, the way Jesus commands and intends? It is the way He designed for our flourishing. It is the way He designed for our best method of loving God and neighbor with our speech.

Jesus' simple living relates to not just His actions, but also His character. Jesus' simplicity is seen in His humility. He "emptied himself, taking the form of a servant," Philippians 2:7. Humility is simple, though it can be difficult. There are many good quotes on humility, but I have long defined it as realizing God is God and you are not, that you are creature/created, and living in light of that reality. Only God Himself is perfectly humble. But simple living can assist your learning humility and humility will assist your simple living. I have been an arrogant, grasping person. I have needed a Jesus-style simple living to help me love Him and my neighbors better. I continue to need it.

Jesus' simple living includes the fact that He focuses on the things that matter most. He invites the lost into the family of God. He trains the believers. He has mercy on the hurting (e.g., the sick, the paralyzed, the possessed, the grieving). He gave us the task of inviting the lost into the family of God and then training those who would believe (Matt. 28:18-20). He also illustrated for us that He wants us to continue His mercy ministry (Matt. 25:40). We can sometimes confuse ourselves into paralysis with moral dilemmas. But the ethics of Jesus are incredibly simple.

Jesus taught us that God is our provider, so we need worry for nothing (Luke 12:22-34; Mt. 6). We need to do our own work (2 Thessalonians 3:10), but God will provide. Everything we have, including the things we bought and paid for with our salary, are provided by God (James 1:17). Holding this perspective helps keep us humble. It helps us remember we can live simply, without all the excesses that culture would have us vainly pursue.

Jesus sacrificed His time. He had mercy on the crowds after John the Baptist's death, which led to the famous feeding of the five thousand. In Matthew 14:12, Jesus learns of His cousin's death. Verse 13 reports that He sought solitude, but the crowds followed and approached Him for healing. He chose to sacrifice His time and His feelings in order to serve those in need. Are Christians exempt from following Jesus' example? Surely not.

Jesus sacrificed (and taught us to sacrifice) earthly relationships if they rejected faith in Christ. Now, *a word of caution is due for this subject*. We live in an age of cancel culture and "going no contact" with people. We live in a divisive and angry age. These things are not of God. We must not let ourselves be ruled by foolishness, anger, or hatred. Let's look at the passages and then talk in more detail.

In Matthew 12:46-50, Jesus prioritizes the family of faith over His biological family. When the people tell Him His family is outside and wish to speak with Him, Jesus replies with the question, "Who is my mother and who are my brothers?" In verse 50, He goes on to answer His own question, "Whoever does the will of my Father in heaven is my brother and sister and mother." Earlier, in Matthew 10, we see a lot of instructions for how the disciples are to go on mission. He clarified the sacrificial nature of committing to Christ. It involves true faith, which will inevitably divide believer from unbeliever. Matthew 10:32-39 says, "Therefore, everyone who will acknowledge me before others, I will also acknowledge him before my Father in heaven. But whoever denies me before others, I will also deny him before my Father in heaven. Don't assume that I came to bring peace on the earth. I did not come to bring peace, but a sword. For I came to turn

a man against his father,

a daughter against her mother,
a daughter-in-law against her mother-in-law;

and a man's enemies will be
the members of his household.

The one who loves a father or mother more than me is not worthy of me; the one who loves a son or daughter more than me is not worthy of me. And whoever doesn't take up his cross and follow me is not worthy of me. Anyone who finds his life will lose it, and anyone who loses his life because of me will find it."

Christians are people who want to lose our lives for Christ's sake ("because of me") so that we can find our lives again. They are found in Christ Himself. So, yes, there may be times we have to face tough choices. It is extremely hard for some Christians to be Christians because they come from a family of people who are strong in their faith in a false god. They may be criticized, verbally abused, persecuted, or shunned for their faith in Christ. Sacrificial living at a small scale helps us understand and be ready for sacrificial living at a larger scale.

Remember James 1:19-20, "Know this, my beloved brothers: let every person be quick to hear, slow to speak, slow to anger; for the anger of man does not produce the righteousness of God."

We don't look for reasons to be angry with our unbelieving neighbors, friends, or relatives. We give up the anger of man so we can choose the way of Christ. Truth in love. God's peace, which surpasses all understanding. We embrace Jesus, who though He was mistreated and persecuted, did not respond in kind (1 Peter 2:23).

But on a smaller scale, there will be times our unbelieving family or friends wants us to do something like get high. Or watch a major Hollywood movie that happens to have nudity or other pornographic content in it. Or they want to gossip. We must tell them in love, "No." We sacrifice such activities because it is not the way of Christ. Some people will accept our answer. Some people will not. We have to trust God with ALL those people, and all those relationships.

Jesus ultimately sacrificed on the cross! Jesus died so that all who believe in Him will not perish, but have eternal life (John 3:16). His death on the cross is the biggest way in which Jesus chose a sacrificial life and it is the best example for choosing a sacrificial life. While we

Christians do not die for others as their savior, we do emulate Him. We walk the path Jesus walked as we have opportunity to lay something down for the sake of others. We lay down our time, our energy. We lay down our laziness, or our arrogance. We lay down whatever is not of God so that we can take up whatever is HIS and offer to one another.

"Like the Pony Express, serving God is not a job for the casually interested. It's costly service. God asks for your life. He requires that service to Him become a priority, not a pastime." -Donald S. Whitney

Living a simple life, as we talked about earlier, is not the same as living on a farm in the country. That's not what we mean. Living simply means living without duplicity, as alluded to in the quote from Richard Foster at the beginning of this chapter. James 1:5-8 says, "Now if any of you lacks wisdom, he should ask God—who gives to all generously and ungrudgingly—and it will be given to him. But let him ask in faith without doubting. For the doubter is like the surging sea, driven and tossed by the wind. That person should not expect to receive anything from the Lord, *being double-minded* and unstable in all his ways." Or, to go back to a verse we discussed before,

Matthew 6:24 reports Jesus' words, "No one can serve two masters, since either he will hate one and love the other, or he will be devoted to one and despise the other. You cannot serve both God and money."

There is no flourishing coming your way if you engage in both the double-minded, split-attention, syncretistic worship of Jesus of Nazareth AND your ego, or the pursuit of money, etc. You will not be the human being God designed and called you to be if you live that way.

Just as simple living does not mean country living, it also does not mean ignorant or lazy living. We are called to know the Lord. He is knowable! He has made Himself known through the Bible. And so we are called to study and know God's Word so we might better know *Him*. Simple living does not mean "never study the Word." It does not mean "read for 2 minutes," nor does it mean "consider reading a single-verse Instagram post as your daily Bible reading". You don't have to get a PhD from a seminary, but you are called to the renewal of your mind! Give God your best by trying to dig every treasure out of the Word that you possibly can! Remember the parable of the treasure buried in a field (Matthew 13:44). "The kingdom of heaven is like treasure, buried in a field, that a man found and reburied. Then in his joy he goes and sells everything he has and buys that field." Dig, and dig, and dig again! There is SO MUCH to be found that will bless your life. Simple living is not intentional ignorance.

"[Christians who seek God's kingdom first] easily put all demands that come to them in 'their place' and deal harmoniously, peacefully, and confidently with complexities of life that seem incomprehensible to others, for they know what they are doing. In the spiritual life, simplicity is not opposed to complexity, and poverty is not opposed to possessions. In fact, as simplicity makes great complexity bearable, so poverty as Bonhoeffer explains it—freedom from desire—makes possessions safe and fruitful for the glory of God."[9]

Simple living is an active choice NOT to pursue the love of money or piling up earthly treasures. It is a choice not to make ourselves so busy that we never have time for God or our neighbors. Let me restate that last sentence in a positive way. It is a choice to make ourselves available daily, weekly, monthly, to the time

---

[9] Dallas Willard, *The Spirit of the Disciplines*, 205.

needed for us to love God well and to love our neighbors well. As you do so, you will find yourself engaging not only simple living, but sacrificial living, too.

Let me give you one more quote from Richard Foster. I won't apologize for quoting him so much on this subject! He's the best writer I've read on it.

"The central point for the Discipline of simplicity is to seek the kingdom of God and the righteousness of his kingdom *first* and then everything necessary will come in its proper order. It is impossible to overestimate the importance of Jesus' insight at this point. Everything hinges upon maintaining the 'first' thing as first. Nothing must come before the kingdom of God, including the desire for a simple life-style." (Emphasis in original.)

In closing, Willard has a fittingly concise definition of simple living. In his words, simple living is "the arrangement of life around a few consistent purposes, explicitly excluding what is not necessary to human well-being."[10]

---

[10] Willard, 170.

CHAPTER 5: SERVICE TO OTHERS

"WANTED: Gifted volunteers for difficult service in the local expression of the kingdom of God. Motivation to serve should be obedience to God, gratitude, gladness, forgiveness, humility, and love. Service will rarely be glorious. Volunteers must be faithful in spite of long hours, little or no visible results, and possibly no recognition—except from God for all eternity." -Donald S. Whitney

The biblical witness regarding salvation is very simple. Believe in Jesus as the Christ, the Son of God. By believing, you will have life in his name (John 20:13). We are saved by grace through faith, not through works, so that nobody can boast (Ephesians 2:8-9). That is, we are saved from the consequences of our sin, which is death (Romans 6:23). We are saved by grace, or in other words, by God's free gift (also Romans 6:23). That grace is delivered to us through faith (Eph. 2:8-9; Rom. 10:4, 9-10).

Many theologians and pastors have remarked that, in all the religions of the world, there are truly only two concepts for how people are saved from sin. One concept is the Christian concept, expressed to us clearly in the Scriptures, that we are saved through faith in

Christ. The other concept, which is ultimately the concept of salvation in every other faith and worldview, is that people are saved by works. Some things can be true at the same time. When people ask who you are, you can tell them your name, but it is also accurate to tell them what you do for a living, or who you are in relation to your family. But a theology of salvation (soteriology) does not work like that. Only one can be true, and not the other.

Why do I bring this up? In this chapter, we are talking about service and I want to be sure to communicate that Christians serve BECAUSE we are saved from sin, NOT IN ORDER TO BE saved from sin. Christians do not trust in our own works to save us or make our presence in the future state palatable to a perfectly holy God. No. We trust in the work of Christ, whose work was to die on the cross and then to rise to resurrected life on the third day. A preacher I know recently preached a series of sermons called "SAVED TO SERVE." I think that sums it up very well.

Let's talk about how we can learn about the spiritual discipline of service from the life of Jesus, starting with that most important part of it.

Jesus' purpose on this earth was to live a perfect life, die for us, and rise again. That is service! It is service on behalf of all who will believe. There are some elements to notice about this act of service from Jesus.

1. **This act of service cost Jesus personally.** Notice, he did not send someone else. God Himself died on the cross for our sins, not a man, angel, or animal.

2. **This act of service was for the benefit of others.** You may rightfully point out that all service is for the benefit of others. But among sinful man, motives, means, and results can be debated endlessly. Jesus' death, burial, and resurrection, however, concludes debates. He lives again on the other side of death. There can be no argument in the face of the King of Kings. His service was to the benefit of all who will believe. Our faith in Him would mean nothing if He did not die and rise again (1 Corinthians 15).

3. **This act of service was motivated out of Jesus' love and joy.** Jesus' twin motivations of love and joy for us is

clearly seen in the Scriptures. Romans 5:8, "But God proves his own love for us in that while we were still sinners, Christ died for us." Love was on display on the cross in the bloodied form of that Jewish rabbi. But look also to Hebrews 12:2b as it comments on Jesus' motivation. "For the joy that lay before him, he endured the cross, despising the shame, and sat down at the right hand of the throne of God." Reuniting us to Himself gives Jesus joy just like the joy of the angels that Jesus described in Luke 15, verses 7 and 10. How could His joy in our salvation be any less than that?

4. **This act of service was conducted not only out of righteous motivations, but also righteous means**. Please don't misunderstand me. The persecutions of the religious leaders, bloodthirsty crowds, and dangerously apathetic Romans were not righteous. What we see in Jesus' sacrificial act of service on the cross is a man who did not sin at any point along the way. He was pierced because of our acts of rebellion against God (Is. 53:5), not His own. And when He suffered the betrayal,

trials, and crucifixion, "he was oppressed and afflicted, yet he did not open his mouth" (Is. 53:7). The eyewitness Simon Peter, son of Jonah, declares in 1 Peter 2:22-24 about Jesus, "He did not commit sin, and no deceit was found in his mouth; when he was insulted, he did not insult in return; when he suffered, he did not threaten but entrusted himself to the one who judges justly. He himself bore our sins in his body on the tree; so that, having died to sins, we might live for righteousness. By his wounds you have been healed."

So much could be said about the crucifixion and resurrection of Jesus, but the above paragraphs should suffice for our study on the spiritual disciplines. Let's turn to the second clearest picture of Jesus and service with help from the Gospel of John.

A look at John 13 allows us to move the camera from Jesus' death and resurrection to the night just before Jesus' betrayal by Judas. Picture the scene in your imagination. It's been another long day, a day of walking and dust and sweat. Preparations had been made to borrow the upper room of somebody's home. They were planning and expecting to observe the Passover. But there was no servant there to get them ready. These men *needed* to be ceremonially clean in order to engage in the observation of Passover! Even so, there was nobody to kneel down with a towel and basin of water in order to wash and dry their feet. This kind of job was a dirty job. It would have featured on one of Mike Rowe's TV shows if they had existed back then. It was unenviable, time-consuming, perhaps humiliating to wash the grime and potentially animal feces off the feet of whoever was coming to dinner. The washing of feet is a job for a servant.

Jesus, the King of Creation, who has the Name Above All Names, the One who knew He would die in less than 24 hours, knelt, took up the towel, and did it Himself. He washed the feet of the twelve disciples and, presumably, His own. Judas, then, the famous traitor who would hand Jesus over for thirty pieces of silver, was among this number. Can you imagine washing the feet of someone who betrayed you? Jesus did that. He did it before the betrayal, yes, but He did it knowing that the betrayal would happen. And don't forget Peter's betrayal! Peter would hang back from Jesus' side as his master was brought before the kangaroo court we see in the Gospels. When pressed by the people nearby whether he was one of Jesus' disciples, he cussed and insisted he did not know the man! Jesus knew Peter's betrayal was coming and Jesus washed *his* feet, too.

In the context of another prophetic pronouncement of His coming betrayal and crucifixion, Jesus famously declared in Mark 10:45, "For even the Son of Man did not come to be served, but to serve, and to give his life as a ransom for many." Matthew's account of that same moment reflects these words on Christians and service. Matt. 20:25-28, "Whoever would be great among you must be your servant . . . even as the Son of Man came not to be served but to serve."

"That's all well and good for Jesus," you might be thinking, "but that has nothing to do with me." My friend, if that is what you think, you are mistaken. We are to follow Jesus, just as the first disciples were called to do (Matt. 4:19).

John 13:14-15 record these words from Jesus. "If I then, your Lord and Teacher, have washed your feet, you also ought to wash one another's feet. For I have given you an example, that you also should do as I have done to you." Some of you reading this may come from a congregation or a denomination that regularly holds foot washing services on an annual or more frequent basis. For those who are unfamiliar, some churches hold a service where they plan and then conduct a time where those in attendance have the opportunity to wash the feet of another person in attendance. It is a humbling experience. My point is not to argue that your church should have a service like this. The point is to show that Jesus' life is characterized by personal service done on behalf of others and so ours should be characterized by the same.

"In the Discipline of service there is also great liberty. Service enables us to say 'no!' to the world's games of promotion and authority. It abolishes our need (and desire) for a 'pecking order.'" -Richard Foster

If Jesus' acts of service were personal, ours need to be personal, as well. We live in a digital age. We live in the age of drive thru everything from food to coffee shops, banks, and more. We live in a world that we have shaped in our own image. We have curated online church with music from *this* church, preaching from *that* church, inspirational videos from our favorite Christian influencers, and we call that the Christian life. Meanwhile, we lay back and are spiritually gluttonous. We feed and feed and feed on only the morsels we choose, neglecting those dynamics of the Christian life we prefer to avoid or the books and passages of the Bible the challenge us or make us uncomfortable. We prefer not to put up with the bad smells of the bodies of other people. We prefer not to deal with their (in our opinion) bad driving or bad parking. We prefer not to use a (gasp) public restroom. We prefer not to walk down the street, or drive a few minutes, or catch a bus in order to attend a worship service. "Online church" is not what God had in mind. We are embodied souls! We need to spend time in spaces with one another singing, reading, praying, and, yes, performing service to others. We need to do it ourselves. We cannot outsource service to somebody else. We have to use our own hands to lift the fallen. We have to use our own feet to go to the outcast. We have to use our own ears to listen to the cries of the grieving. We have to use our own voices to encourage the downcast. We have to use our own backs to bear the burdens of one another.

If Jesus' acts of service were for the benefit of others, ours need to be for the benefit of others, too. On social media, there is almost no content worth reading or viewing. Among all the fluff of wasted time are videos of people who feed the homeless or helping a family experiencing poverty. There are so many of those videos that now there are parody videos mocking them! We do not serve in order to be seen. Matthew 6:2, "Be careful not to practice your righteousness in front of others to be seen by them. Otherwise, you have no reward with your Father in heaven." You may notice the Scripture address there and remember that it comes from the Sermon on the Mount. Jesus also said this in the same sermon, "In the same way, let your light shine before others, so that they may see your good works and give glory to your Father in heaven" (Mt. 5:16). We best serve when we do it in ways that causes people see the good works, not us, and give glory to the Father, not to us.

If Jesus' acts of service were motivated from love and joy for others, so ours need to be, as well. Do you remember the Greatest Commandments? They come into play with regards to everything we do, including our acts of service. Love God, love people (Luke 10:27-28). Love—real love, not the cheap, uncommitted, convenient kind of appreciation that so commonly passes for love nowadays—and joy go together. Read your Bible, pray, and develop your love for God and others. Don't hold back from service simply because you think you don't love people enough, though! Sometimes, it is through our acts of service that we mature in our love for God and others. Charles Spurgeon preached a sermon titled *Some Marks of God's People*. In it, he stated, "He who serves God, out of love to him, is the one who really and truly serves him. The Lord of love, the great King eternal, immortal, invisible, needs no slaves to grace his throne. He wants those to do his bidding who serve him with delight and pleasure."

<u>If Jesus' acts of service were conducted via righteous means, then we need to do the same.</u> Service must be done with a joyful, loving motivation, but also a joyful, loving means. Imagine a children's ministry volunteer serving preschool kids with a scowl on his face. (Depending on your church experiences, it might not be too hard to imagine!) Such things should not be. We conduct our acts of service with love, not lashes. Sometimes, we can serve in such a way that we never voice negative words, but our posture, demeanor, facial expression, and other elements communicate a bad attitude anyway. It is not the way of Jesus. James 1:20, "for human anger does not accomplish God's righteousness." I am not telling you to force yourself to "feel like serving." Nor am I saying to "only serve when you feel like it". (You will soon come to a place where you NEVER feel like it, which is not the way of Jesus.) What I mean is, develop self-control, that flavor of the Fruit of the Spirit. Let God be in charge, and in submission to him take control of your face, body language, and any other element that communicates to people so that you can serve in such a way that they are blessed rather than more burdened.

I want to close this chapter with some bite-size thoughts on practical service and even one of its benefits, followed by one more quote.

Service does not care whether the task is large or small. Service is content to serve in hidden ways, not in the spotlight. Service is free not to calculate every result. Service is happy to minister to all, great or small, poor or rich, etc. Service ministers simply and faithfully, regardless of mood or feelings. Service is a pattern of life, not limited to one or two instances. Service builds community.

"Therefore, the spiritual authority of Jesus is an authority not found in a position or a title, but in a towel," Richard Foster.

CHAPTER 6: GATHERING FOR WORSHIP

"Some Christians try to go to heaven alone, in solitude. But believers are not compared to bears or lions or other animals that wander alone. Those who belong to Christ are sheep in this respect, that they love to get together. Sheep go in flocks, and so do God's people."
-Charles Spurgeon

In this chapter, I want us to continue to look at the spiritual disciplines by looking at the subject of worship. Earlier, I broadly defined the spiritual disciplines as the same as a good faith attempt to follow Jesus. More specifically, I said that it is **"following Jesus in the overall style of life He chose for Himself."** Jesus chose a life of attending corporate (i.e., gathered) worship services in order to focus on and respond to God. Can Christians learn something about going to church from Jesus? That's a great question! Thank you for asking. The answer is both "yes" and "no." I want to dispel some mistaken conceptions with the "no" side of the answer, and I want to show you just some of the riches of what the Bible has to say on the "yes" side of the answer. We will start with the shorter list of those two, but before that, let's briefly define worship.

I think Donald S. Whitney defines worship well in his book *Spiritual Disciplines for the Christian Life*. He writes, "Worship often includes words and actions, but it goes beyond them to the focus of the mind and heart. Worship is the God-centered focus and response of the soul; it is being preoccupied with God. So no matter what you are saying or singing or doing at any moment, you are worshiping God only when He is the center of your attention. But whenever you do focus on the infinite worth of God, you will respond in worship as surely as the moon reflects the sun."[11] Worship is certainly much, much more than singing songs to God. Worship can be changing your baby's diaper. It can be a moment of reflection and prayer before you step into your place of work. It can be the washing of the dishes at the end of a long day. Worship can be more than singing and reading God's Word and responding to what God's Word tells you in a sermon, but it is certainly not less than that.

Christians cannot learn about going to church from Jesus *if by that you consider church to be*

---

[11] Donald S. Whitney, *Spiritual Disciplines for the Christian Life* (Colorado Springs, CO: NavPress, 2014), 106.

a kind of service industry that tunes up the tires and engines of your spiritual vehicle. Churches are not interchangeable entities that simply perform the same functions at higher or lower levels of efficiency. Allow me an analogy here. In my neighborhood, we have two Jack in the Box locations. (Very spiritual example, I know.) One Jack in the Box has a perfectly fine track record with me and my family. We get what we pay for. The staff there are professional and timely. The other Jack in the Box has a staff member who has engaged, on multiple occasions, in short-changing our order, demanding we pay him after the fact for things we spoke aloud in our order, and has openly rudely criticized us ("you should have said you wanted that when you first made your order"). I'm not perfect, but I'm also not interested in getting into it with that manager. I simply don't want to do business at that location any more, so I don't. I get the exact same products at the other location, but I also get them accurately and without undue criticism. It is a worldly—or, really, a biblically ignorant—way of thinking to consider a church to function like any other business. It is worldly to think the church needs to fit everything I want out of a church. It needs to have a great preacher, great music, a beautiful place to meet, hot coffee when I show up to service, and it better only have smiling faces of people who have no problems. And if those people do have problems, well, they better have nothing to do with me. But church is not a fast food place or an auto shop. Church is family. Church is a gathering of God's people. The gathering of God's people is meant to glorify God, not you. The gathering of God's people is to make God known, to encourage one another, to serve as a hospital for the broken, not as a beautiful museum for the saints. If we think church is an American corporation we can simply change for another at our whim or convenience, then no, we can learn nothing about this from the life of Jesus.

"When a Christian shuns fellowship with other Christians, the devil smiles. When he stops studying the Bible, the devil laughs. When he stops praying, the devil shouts for joy." -Corrie Ten Boom

Jesus does, however, show us life in the gathered community of God's people. Jesus participated in the weekly gathering of corporate worship. Luke 4 records Jesus' rejection in Nazareth, but the context of that rejection occurs around Jesus reading and expounding on the scroll of Isaiah at the synagogue. For our purposes, the most relevant verse is 16, which says, "He came to Nazareth, where he had been brought up. *As usual*, he entered the synagogue on the Sabbath day and stood up to read" (emphasis added). A more literal translation using the Greek word order would read, "... He entered according to the custom of his on the day of the Sabbath..." The phrase "as usual" (or, "according to his custom") translates κατὰ (according to) τὸ (the) εἰωθὸς (custom) αὐτῷ (his).[4] I highlight the Greek phrasing here in order to show that the phrase "as usual" or "according to his custom" is not an addition by a modern translator or editor. The Gospels tell us Jesus' habit was to attend the weekly worship service at His local synagogue. Psalm 95:6 says, "Come, let's worship and bow down; let's kneel before the Lord our Maker." Picture what that looked like when Jesus obeyed that directive in the synagogue in Nazareth and when He was in the temple in Jerusalem. God expects us to worship. Jesus did just that.

If the Bible reports that the perfectly holy, perfectly loving God the Son attended the weekly gathering of God's people, then the Bible has something to say to mankind in all periods of history, but especially to us in the age of so-called online church or the myopic practices of individualistic Christianity.

"The single most important activity of your life is to worship God. You were *made for this*—to offer your *whole* life, in *all* its parts, as a hymn of praise to the Lord." -Sinclair Ferguson

Jesus' participation in the weekly worship service of God's people shows that it is a necessity, not mere tradition or cultural preference. Notice that Jesus spends a lot of time with His disciples and that the disciples spend a lot of time with one another. These decisions are not accidents or coincidences. These gatherings, these times of worship, are part of the design. Jesus sang hymns with His disciples at the conclusion of their Passover observance, aka the Last Supper, before they went out to the Garden of Gethsemane in Matt. 26:30. Jesus read the Isaiah scroll and expounded on it in Luke 4, as referenced above. But He also would have stayed silent and listened as others did so when it was their turn.

"Be united with other Christians. A wall with loose bricks is not good. The bricks must be cemented together." -Corrie Ten Boom

We know Jesus focused on and responded to God in a variety of moments, but I want to encourage you not to miss the night leading up to Jesus' betrayal by Judas. All four Gospels record that moment from various perspectives. Luke 22:42 records an incredible moment in Jesus' worship through prayer that night. In it, Jesus prays, "Father, if you are willing, take this cup away from me—nevertheless, not my will, but yours, be done." Truly, this response to God is the best response to God. May it be true of you and I that we respond to Him in that same way every day.

"To gather with God's people in united adoration of the Father is as necessary to the Christian life as prayer." -Martin Luther

Christians today can follow Jesus' example in the spiritual disciplines by engaging in daily private worship and public worship at least once a week. (Your church may have more than one opportunity to worship together.) Make no mistake: you must have both regular private and public worship in order to best follow Jesus. He deserves our best, but you know what? You deserve your best, too. Engage in daily private times of reading the Bible and praying. Maybe play a worship song on your phone that you can sing along to. But don't stay isolated! Make sure you at least attend your local church's worship service in person every week, unless you are limited by distance, illness, or mobility. You need it. May we not be indifferent to the regular, disciplined worship of God! May what Hebrews 12:28 says also be true of us, "Therefore let us be grateful for receiving a kingdom that cannot be shaken, and thus let us offer to God acceptable worship, with reverence and awe" (ESV).

I want to close this chapter with a quote from A.W. Tozer. He said, "If you will not worship God seven days a week, you do not worship Him on one day a week."[12]

---

[12] John Blanchard, ed., *More Gathered Gold: A Treasury of Quotations for Christians* (Welwyn, England: Evangelical Press, 1986), 344.

CHAPTER 7: STEWARDSHIP

"Don't tell me you're trusting God until you trust Him with your pocketbook." -J. Vernon McGee

You may be surprised to hear that we can learn about the discipline of stewardship from the life of Jesus. Jesus kept the Law perfectly, unlike any of the rest of us. That means he kept the Law with regards to stewardship perfectly. Jesus was a perfect steward. If we can see anything about this area of life from Him, then we will see a perfect example to follow.

First, we should define stewardship. Stewardship is a person's management of resources that are owned by somebody else. The manager of your local Wal-Mart stewards the goods sold at his or her store, while the Walton family and various shareholders own those goods. Stewardship can be done well or poorly. Whether done well or poorly, it is the management of those resources. Stewardship began in Genesis 1:28 (see also, Gen. 2:15-16).

I have some encouraging news for you. You only have two things to steward in your life! I can hear your relief already. A list of two items? That is a sweet deal. One of the items you steward is your time. The other item you steward is every asset God puts in your life. Ok, so, maybe things are slightly more complicated than two items. But it really does come down to those two things. We have time and we have resources. Some of those resources are money, yes, but we also have our physical body, our various possessions (clothes, personal items), utility items (groceries, tools), skills, experiences, training, as well as our relationships with family, friends, co-workers, fellow church members, and neighbors. I don't know about you, but I have found it encouraging to realize that everything God put in my life is something He has trusted me to care for in ways that honor Him and in ways that best manage that resource.

With regards to how we spend our time, Jesus said some very important things. Matthew 6:33, "But seek first the kingdom of God and his righteousness, and all these things will be provided for you." If you are seeking God's kingdom and His righteousness first, that will have a measurable and significant impact on how you steward your time! You will prioritize daily private time with God in prayer. You will prioritize knowing what it is God said! And so you will read the Bible regularly. You will prioritize obeying God with your actions, which means you will spend time "doing the do's" and not so much "doing the don'ts".

John 9:4-5 records Jesus saying, "We must do the works of him who sent me while it is day. Night is coming when no one can work. As long as I am in the world, I am the light of the world." On a related note, Jesus calls Christians the light of the world in the Sermon on the Mount (Matt. 5:14). Jesus is not in the world right now because He is at the right hand of the Father, but we ARE in the world! And we are the body of Christ. So we must do the works of God while there is still time. The clock is ticking. Jesus will return someday, which will be the end of our work. Many have attempted to predict that day and time, to their embarrassment (Mark 13:32). None of us will ever know it in advance. But when the end comes, the time for evangelism and missions will end. We've got to share the Gospel while there is still time!

Jesus also spoke to stewarding time in Luke 9. At the end of that chapter, we read three accounts of people saying they will follow Jesus. The final brief account is Luke 9:61-62, which says, "Another said, 'I will follow you, Lord, but first let me go and say good-bye to those at my house.' But Jesus said to him, 'No one who puts his hand to the plow and looks back is fit for the kingdom of God.'" Jesus wants you to follow him. Jesus does not want you to wait while you figure out what you are doing. There are men and women, boys and girls headed towards an eternity separated from God forever in hell. There is no time for you to claim to want to be in the kingdom of God, while looking back on your life in the kingdom of Satan as something to gaze upon. John 3:14-15, "Just as Moses lifted up the snake in the wilderness, so the Son of Man must be lifted up, so that everyone who believes in him may have eternal life." We are to continually be "keeping our eyes on Jesus, the source and perfecter of our faith" (Hebrews 12:2a). Just as those who were poisoned looked on the image Moses lifted up (Numbers 21:4-9), we are to look on Jesus Christ. We put our hand to the plow and we get to work. That kind of conduct is a discipline. You don't stumble into it and you don't engage in it sporadically.

Jesus had a lot to say about money. I know it is a popular thought that "you don't talk about money." People think any Christian writer, thinker, or pastor who talks about money is just greedy. I feel sorry for people who think that way. None of the pastors I have served under are greedy and I am so grateful for their example. Jesus had a lot more to say about money than you might guess. If you were to count up the number of teachings or number of verses from the four Gospels and compare how many times Jesus spoke about money versus how much He spoke about other subjects, you might be surprised to see that it is one of the top subjects He addressed. When I read the Bible and I see how much He had to say about finances, I am increasingly comforted and encouraged that it actually is a normal and, in fact, good thing to think about and talk about so that we can manage finances to the best of our ability.

Jesus taught through the Parable of the Talents (Matthew 25:14-30), for example. In that parable, He taught about how God wants us to utilize our resources to the best of our ability. You were given that resource to use it, not hide it!

Jesus taught through another parable, about The Unforgiving Servant (Matthew 18:21-35). The primary point of that passage is about forgiveness in general, and readers would do well to always remember that. At the same time, we can learn about the ugliness of greed and the beauty of repenting from that kind of greed in that parable.

"He that trusts in the Lord has found out the way to handle matters wisely, and happy is he."
-Charles Spurgeon

Parables are indirect teaching, but Jesus also taught directly on the issue of stewardship. In His direct teaching, he dealt with both resources and time.

In and after his encounter with the Rich Young Ruler (Matthew 19:16-30), Jesus speaks to the issue of financial stewardship. We see in His teaching one way in which it is difficult for those who hoard wealth. Matthew 19:23-24, "Jesus said to his disciples, 'Truly I tell you, it will be hard for a rich person to enter the kingdom of heaven. Again I tell you, it is easier for a camel to go through the eye of a needle than for a rich person to enter the kingdom of God.'" Riches may buy the nice house, the slick car, the tastiest foods, and the flashiest clothes, but it will not buy you entrance to God's eternal presence as a member of His family. Only your faith determines whether you are in the kingdom or not. As Christians, we already know this truth, but we would do well to be disciplined in our relationship to money.

Jesus speaks to our relationship with money very famously in Matthew 6:24, "No one can serve two masters, since either he will hate one and love the other, or he will be devoted to one and despise the other. You cannot serve both God and money." We must know and we must have the discipline towards money that God calls us to. Money is a tool, but it is only one of many. It is not worth pursuing as your highest calling. It is not worth worrying over when the economy gets worse, or when you have to give up a few "wants" from your monthly budget. It isn't even worth worrying about with regards to your needs! Philippians 4:6 says, "Don't worry about anything, but in everything through prayer and petition with thanksgiving, present your requests to God." Jesus made this same point in the Sermon on the Mount immediately following the verse I quoted at the beginning of this paragraph (Matt. 6:25-34).

I recognize that this is easier to say than to do. I, myself, am still embedding this truth deeper down into my mind and soul. But that which is true is always true, even when it is a difficult truth to handle.

"The Bible does not portray the faithful follower of Jesus as a person who never tastes anxiety or fear. Rather, the Bible portrays anxiety and fear as something that rises unbidden in the heart and must be dealt with from a Christian perspective, a Christian approach, a Christian way." -John Piper

As the one who kept the Law, Jesus would have tithed. It was taught in passages like Leviticus 27:30-33; Numbers 18:21-32; Deuteronomy 14:22-29, and Deut. 26:2-15. God's plan for finances among the people of God includes our giving Him the first ten percent of our income. He does this not because He needs the help, but because Christians need the help. We need help trusting God. We need help with means of showing a watching world that we trust God. We need help with the self-discipline to not let money rule over us, but for God-with-us to rule money through us. Again, you cannot serve both God and money. Choose this day who you will serve!

One flavor of the Fruit of the Spirit (Galatians 5:22-23) is that of self-control. One of the expressions of Spirit-born self-control in your life will be your stewardship of the time and resources you have at your disposal. He gave you today. He gave you lungs that breathe and a heart that beats. He gave you every moment and every resource you have. Will you hide and hoard your time and resources? Or will you trust God? Will you keep all your time and resources as a slothful expression of self-obsession? Or will you give away what you can in order to engage in God's mission to seek and to save the lost? Matthew 16:24-25, "Then Jesus said to his disciples, 'If anyone wants to follow after me, let him deny himself, take up his cross, and follow me. For whoever wants to save his life will lose it, but whoever loses his life because of me will find it.'"

Develop the discipline for utilizing your time, talents, and treasure as a faithful steward of the Lord God. Don't waste them. Don't let them rule you. Let God rule and you follow.

CHAPTER 8: CONFESSION OF SIN

"But that does not mean that confession is a light and easy thing, a simple mouthing of words, a verbal ritual. Mere admission is not confession. We dishonor Christ by a frivolous view of confession that fails to appreciate how much our sin cost Him. Although not a spiritual self-flagellation, biblical confession does involve at least some degree of grief for the sin committed." -Donald S. Whitney

This book is written to introduce and discuss the spiritual disciplines, most especially through looking at the life and sayings of Jesus. I defined the spiritual disciplines as **"following Jesus in the overall style of life He chose for Himself**." This task has been straight-forward as we discussed prayer and solitude, Bible reading, and simple living. In this chapter, we come to a more difficult subject to glean from Jesus' life. We are talking about confession of sin.

"Without the cross the Discipline of confession would be only psychologically therapeutic. But it is so much more. It involves an objective change in our relationship with God and a subjective change in us. It is a means of healing and transforming the inner spirit." - Richard J. Foster[13]

The reason confession of sin is a difficult spiritual discipline to discuss from the life of Jesus is simply because Jesus never had sin to confess! Jesus was morally perfect (Hebrews 4:15; 1 Peter 2:22).

If the spiritual disciplines are **"following Jesus in the overall style of life He chose for Himself**," can there be a spiritual discipline that Jesus never seemed to need? That is another great question, reader. Thank you for asking!

Jesus spent most of His time in community. In those times, we do find Him doing certain things that connect with this subject. Let me back up and quote Dallas Willard, who said, "In [the spiritual discipline of confession] we let trusted others know our deepest weaknesses and failures. This will nourish our faith in God's provision for our needs through his people, our sense of being loved, and our humility before our brothers and sisters. Thus we let some friends in Christ know who we really are, not holding back anything important, but, ideally, allowing complete transparency. We lay down the burden of hiding and pretending, which

---

[13] Foster, *Celebration of Discipline*, 144.

normally takes up such a dreadful amount of human energy. We engage and are engaged by others in the most profound depths of the soul."[14]

When we understand confession better, with the help of big brother Dallas Willard, we can better see the connection between the life of Jesus and the discipline of confession. What else could the three-year block of training for the twelve disciples be other than Jesus revealing His identity to its deepest level?

The discipline of confession is a Christian revealing the profound depths of his or her soul to a trusted brother or sister. The difference between our confessing and Jesus' confessing is that our confessions include sin.

"When I admonish men to come to confession, I am simply urging them to be Christians." - Martin Luther

God's aim for Christians is to restore relationship with us. If He is in relationship with us, He knows us and we know Him. That is, as is often observed, a vertical angle: God and man, in right relationship. He also designed humanity to be in right relationship with one

---

[14] Willard, *The Spirit of the Disciplines*, 187-188.

another. That is the horizontal angle. We are not meant to be isolated. I am reminded of the famous poem by John Donne, "No Man is an Island." It reads as follows:

No man is an island,

Entire of itself;

Every man is a piece of the continent,

A part of the main.

If a clod be washed away by the sea,

Europe is the less,

As well as if a promontory were:

As well as if a manor of thy friend's

Or of thine own were.

Any man's death diminishes me,

Because I am involved in mankind.

And therefore never send to know for whom the bell tolls;

It tolls for thee.

For us to remain isolated and unknown, by choice, robs us of the flourishing God designed for us. He designed us to flourish in community.

Dietrich Bonhoeffer speaks to it in this way. "Confession is the God-given remedy for self-deception and self-indulgence. When we confess our sins before a brother-Christian, we are mortifying the pride of the flesh and delivering it up to shame and death through Christ. Then through the word of absolution we rise as new men, utterly dependent on the mercy of God. Confession is thus a genuine part of the life of the saints, and one of the gifts of grace. But if it wrongly used, punishment is bound to ensue. In confession, the Christian is conformed to the death of Christ."[15]

Confession creates a means to a more Christlike character. If our aim is to be those who are **"following Jesus in the overall style of life He chose for Himself,"** then the practical means of achieving that goal are necessary. I have had many conversations with Christians who want to grow as believers. They understand the need to read their Bible and pray and participate in the worship gatherings of the church. But, anecdotally, I see less willingness to be known by other Christians. Leaving this spiritual discipline untried would

---

[15] Dietrich Bonhoeffer, *The Cost of Discipleship*, 289.

be like "leaving money on the table," to use that old saying.

Why do we avoid the discipline of confession?

We fear being known. To be known and yet unloved is terrifying. To be "loved" and unknown is anemic, functionally worthless. So what do we do? We overcome fear with love and trust. We must love and trust the Lord, that He knows what He is doing. We trust that He designed this practice for His glory and our good, and that He did so on purpose. James 5:16a says, "Therefore, confess your sins to one another and pray for one another, so that you may be healed." Confession requires that we trust God, yes, but also that we trust one another. We must trust that other Christians actually do have our best interests at heart.

As scary as it may be and as difficult as it seems, we need confession. Become part of a healthy church. Join as a member. Get to know other Christians in that fellowship. Join a small group or life group, depending on how your church is organized. Trust does take time to build, but do build up your trust in those who show themselves trustworthy. In that context, confess who you are and what you have done. Do not let pride get in your way. Don't harbor secret sins that you can keep as some kind of spiritual parasite. Have more of Christ in your character! Repent, and walk towards Jesus, arm in arm with your Christian brethren. Confession is cleansing, life-giving, and precious.

And when others confess their lives and their sins to you, you must steward that trust well. That information is not for public dissemination. It is also not a reason for you to treat your fellow believer as less-than. You take in that information and you love that person anyway. You do not hold those sins against them. You encourage them to forsake sin and to follow Christ in righteous living (Hebrews 10:24). You celebrate when they experience successes!

"But if we know that the people of God are first a fellowship of sinners, we are freed to hear the unconditional call of God's love and to confess our needs openly before our brothers and sisters. We know that we are not alone in our sin. The fear and pride that cling to us like barnacles cling to others also. We are sinners together. In acts of mutual confession we release the power that heals. Our humanity is no longer denied, but transformed."[16]

---

[16] Foster, *Celebration of Discipline*, 145-146.

CHAPTER 9: CELEBRATION

"Joy does not come to you if you are spiritually passive; rather, joy is cultivated, but joy is cultivated by things you do. And the 'things you do' that cultivate Christlike joy are the Spiritual Disciplines." -Donald S. Whitney

At the beginning of this book, we defined the spiritual disciplines as **"following Jesus in the overall style of life He chose for Himself**." As Christ followers, we accept and aim for the goal that God has destined for us. He told us what that destiny is in Romans 8:29a, "For those he foreknew he also predestined to be conformed to the image of his Son…" We want to look like Christ. But we won't get there through passivity. So, we engage the disciplines of studying the Bible for ourselves, prayer, and times of solitude. We live simply and sacrificially. We steward everything God puts in our lives. We serve others, we gather for worship, and we confess sin one to another. The final discipline to discuss is the discipline of celebration.

I can hear you asking, "Celebration is a spiritual discipline?"

"Celebration heartily done makes our deprivations and sorrows seem small, and we

find in it great strength to do the will of our God because his goodness becomes so real to us."
-Dallas Willard

As alluded to in the quote from Donald S. Whitney that opened this chapter, we do the spiritual disciplines so that we can become more like Christ. We do not practice the disciplines in order to be saved! If you believe in Jesus Christ and have repented of your sins, you are already saved by Jesus' work (delivered by grace, through faith), not your works (Ephesians 2:8-19). Christians do good works not to be saved but because we are saved and because they make us more like Christ. Ephesians 2:10 goes on to say, "For we are his workmanship, created in Christ Jesus for good works, which God prepared ahead of time for us to do." Celebrating God and what God does is as inherent to becoming like Christ as reading the Bible and prayer. While we will look broadly at the Bible on this issue, we also want to answer the question, what can we learn about celebration from the life of Jesus?

We know Jesus celebrated the holy days that God commanded in the Old Testament. These holy days marked God's work in human history to show grace and mercy to His people! We see Jesus and His parents observing the pilgrimage festival of the Passover in Luke 2:41-43. Jesus also observed it at the end of His earthly ministry when He was with His disciples in the upper room just prior to His arrest in the Garden of Gethsemane (Luke 22). Like Passover, we have explicit eyewitness testimony that He observed the Feast of Tabernacles (aka, the Festival of Booths, or Sukkot) in John 7 and 8. We also know He observed one holy day not commanded by God in the Old Testament; specifically, we know He observed Hanukkah, also known as the Festival of Dedication, in John 10.[17] We do not have explicit witness to Jesus observing the other festivals (Pentecost/Feast of Weeks, Day of Atonement/Yom Kippur, etc), but as the only person to ever perfectly keep the Law, we know He observed everything He needed to.[18]

We know Jesus fulfilled the Sabbath, but He also kept the Sabbath. The Pharisees didn't think He did! But He kept it perfectly at a level they did not understand. God designed the Sabbath for our good. We celebrate God on the Sabbath and what He has done! As

---

[17] Hanukkah means "Dedication" or "Consecration."
[18] Since Jesus is without sin, He would have nothing to atone for at Yom Kippur. But I would imagine He participated at least in some way. I can't wait to ask Him what those years were like when I see Him face to face!

Christians in the 21st century, we follow the example of the apostles and the other early Christians, who chose to gather on the Lord's Day (that is, Sunday) for the purposes of Bible reading, prayer, gathered worship, and fellowship with one another.

"Celebration is central to all the Spiritual Disciplines. Without a joyful spirit of festivity the Disciplines become dull, death-breathing tools in the hands of modern Pharisees. Every Discipline should be characterized by carefree gaiety and a sense of thanksgiving." -Richard J. Foster

We see what heaven celebrates in the words of Jesus. If heaven celebrates those things, then we know Jesus does, too, since He is the king of heaven! Luke 15 shows us three incredible pictures on this subject. Each of the three parables there show a picture of something or someone lost who is then found. A lost sheep, a lost dowry coin, and a lost (prodigal) son. In each story, that which was lost is found. The shepherd leaves the flock of 99 to find the lost 1. The woman sweeps the entire house until she finds the coin. The father runs to his returning son! What do all these parables have in common? Jesus uses these stories to show us what heaven celebrates. Heaven celebrates when a lost person is found in Christ! Luke 15:7, "I tell you, in the same way, there will be more joy in heaven over one sinner who repents than over ninety-nine righteous people who don't need repentance." Luke 15:10, "I tell you, in the same way, there is joy in the presence of God's angels over one sinner who repents." While we do not have a record of Jesus commenting on the parable of the lost son afterwards, we know that in the story he tells, the father throws a huge, lavish party to celebrate the return of his beloved son. Do you get it yet? Christians celebrate when sinners are forgiven! When the lost are found! When those who were stained by sin are washed as white as snow by the blood of the Lamb!

In the broader witness of Scripture, we see more blinking arrows pointing to the simple expectation that God's people are those who celebrate what God celebrates. Ecclesiastes 3:4 says there is a time to laugh and a time to dance (among other things). Psalm 95:2 calls to us, "Let us enter his presence with thanksgiving; let us shout triumphantly to him in song." Christians celebrate God!

Psalm 118:24 reminds us to celebrate the simple things God gives. "This is the day the Lord has made; let us rejoice and be glad in it."

We so frequently take for granted "normal" things like waking up to see another day. Or eating another meal. Drinking another cup of coffee, or reading a book for pleasure, the joy of seeing a friend, or the blessings of family. Psalm 118:24 is that reminder to rejoice about those good things that God gives. Do not grumble about the "manna" that God gives you; rejoice over it. It also reminds us that the source of the good gift is God, not our own efforts or bank accounts! 1 Thessalonians 5:18 tells us, "Give thanks in everything; for this is God's will for you in Christ Jesus."

Philippians 4:4 is an encouraging verse that I also find very, very challenging. It says, "Rejoice in the Lord always. I will say it again: Rejoice!" Rejoice ALWAYS? What about when things aren't very good? What about when things are objectively bad? Yes, dear reader. Rejoice even then. Those moments are the ones where rejoicing in the Lord will make the most impact on your own soul. I've walked roads where rejoicing is difficult and even seems impossible. I've had those days, those conversations, those sufferings. Will you let me tell you that I got through those days with far more stability, comfort, and joy when I chose to obey God by rejoicing in Him? I was not always faithful to obey God with joy on those days; don't get me wrong. I've failed like anybody else. God has used my failures to help me see the incredible difference between the days when I rejoice and the days when I don't. Furthermore, the reality of experiencing days where we do not feel like rejoicing is evidence that celebration truly is a *discipline*. It is a structured choice despite our circumstances. Jesus is our leader and example in this discipline. Hebrews 12:2b says, "For the joy that lay before him, he endured the cross, despising the shame, and sat down at the right hand of the throne of God." There is more joy to be had on the other side of the trial. Hang in there and celebrate God!

"Here is one of the most important disciplines of engagement, yet most overlooked and misunderstood. [Celebration] is the completion of worship, for it dwells on the greatness of God as shown in his goodness *to us*. We engage in celebration when we enjoy ourselves, our life, our world, *in conjunction with* our faith and confidence in God's greatness, beauty, and goodness." -Dallas Willard

I opened this chapter with a quote from Donald Whitney. Allow me to close with one. "The time to pursue godliness is now, and the way that God has provided this for those who stand forgiven by grace is through diligence in the Spiritual Disciplines."[19]

---

[19] Whitney, *Spiritual Disciplines for the Christian Life*, 167.

FOR FURTHER READING

- Bonhoeffer, Dietrich. *The Cost of Discipleship*. Touchstone: New York, 1995.

- Foster, Richard. *Celebration of Discipline: The Path to Spiritual Growth*. Third edition. HarperCollins: New York, 1998.

- King, Mason. *Spiritual Disciplines: How to Become a Healthy Christian*. B&H Publishing: Brentwood, TN, 2023.

- Whitney, Donald S. *Spiritual Disciplines for the Christian Life*. NavPress: Colorado Springs, 2014.

- Willard, Dallas. *The Spirit of the Disciplines: Understanding How God Changes Lives*. HarperCollins: New York, 1988.

Made in the USA
Coppell, TX
12 February 2026

71843880R00063